Spikenard
Yvonne Reddick

smith|doorstop

Published 2019 by
Smith|Doorstop Books
The Poetry Business
Campo House
54 Campo Lane
Sheffield S1 2EG

Copyright © Yvonne Reddick 2019
All Rights Reserved

ISBN 978-1-912196-21-0

Designed and Typeset by Utter
Printed by Biddles Books

Smith|Doorstop Books are a member of Inpress: www.inpressbooks.co.uk. Distributed by NBN International, Airport Business Centre, 10 Thornbury Road Plymouth PL6 7PP

The Poetry Business gratefully acknowledges the support of Arts Council England.

Contents

5	Desire Path
6	The May-Tree
7	Firesetter
8	The Bait
10	In Amber
11	Cairning
12	Of the Flesh
13	Of Desire
14	Light, Sweet Crude
17	Muirburn
18	Things My Father Told Me
19	The Oak Husband
20	The Lady and the Unicorn
22	Tamer and Gyrfalcon
23	Peregrines
24	La Pive
25	Wayfarers
26	Spikenard
28	Acknowledgements

Desire Path

Once, we thought we'd find a route around the borders
and feel the bounds dissolve, like sutures in a wound.
So my hands roved the path of your spine, and my lowland mouth
spoke your Highlander surname – tried it on like a ring.

I'd flash you the glance you called *that French look*
as you traced the curve of my back, the contours of my flank,
then I slid my Genevan tongue in your ear: *Je t'aime, moi non plus*,
as if I'd become two speakers who split and merged

as tides braid, then loose, the waters of the Channel.
And my fingers with the quickness of a Hann violinist
kissed your tender palms, the image of your grandfather's –
the one who'd call the foals in his Galway brogue.

Oh, I could ride you for miles in one night, unbitted,
without straying an inch from your bed.

The May-Tree

Your embrace was the Shelter Stone
when the ferns began to unscroll their questions.

You planted a may-tree, and said the whitethorn
could not match the bloom in my cheeks.

By summer, you swore you'd carry me from Edale
to Kielder, to show me the lynx dens.

My vows were the Ring of Steall. I gathered hazel-shells
and painted their insides gold.

We crouched in each other's warmth in a snow-hole,
by the year's turning, but the blizzard smothered our fire.

I kissed your collarbone, but thought of Le Col Maudit.
You gave me sweetbriars, and I crushed them in a press.

Your promises grew to a ring of fly agarics.
My nails gripped your shoulders like harriers' talons.

By the end, all that was left was a may-tree,
unfurling the carrion scent of its petals.

Firesetter

You left me a two-word note. Lying
under our bed was your forgotten lighter.
I ran to the forest and held its flame to a fir cone –

the resiny scales hissed like a Molotov cocktail.
I hurled it over your deer fence
into the spruces where we once heard nightjars.

Three months of drought; those trees were jackstraws.
A flicker in the tinder, bird-call panic.
The easterly sighed on the flames as I walked away.

I pictured your garden: a sheaf of flaming letters
where the paper birch once stood.
The oaks, hands of bone with a furnace backdrop.

Two days in, my brushfire had swallowed fifty hectares.
Sirens through the heat-haze,
villagers were silhouettes with hose reels.

Peat earth: fire skulked underground at a smoulder.
Wheat burned from the root up.
On the third day, a rain of soot. The school stood empty.

Nine days on, fire-crews drained the lake,
the village abandoned under a haze.
The ninth night – I found the staircase

leading to air, the bedroom blasted open,
the ribs and roof-tree smoking.
You stepped from the charred gape of the door.

The Bait
With strangling snare, or windowy net – John Donne

You were two years gone. I swallowed the hook of his smile.
He poured me wine, dark as a wound; wouldn't drink,
but coiled a tattooed arm around my waist.
He said he'd sear a quail's breast for me.

I poured him wine, dark as a wound; wouldn't drink.
When he asked to come to my place, I told him no.
He said he'd sear a quail's breast for me –
he'd turn the flame up high, it would take a few minutes.

When he came to my place, I told him no,
but he had to show me his cooking – I'd be impressed.
He'd turn the flame up high: it would take a few hours.
He caught my wrist. His grip was a snare,

he had to show me his cock – I'd be impressed –
it felt like a bolt-gun, pressing the base of my spine.
He pinioned my arm, his grip was a snare
and my no was the carved-out tongue of a doe.

It felt like a bolt-gun at the base of my spine –
I wrenched free, burst through the door,
my no the carved-out tongue of a doe.
Damn you, long-gone lover, for not breaking his jaw.

I wrenched free, burst through the door –
fuck these numb fists for not breaking his jaw.
My brother: 'You wore jeans – what did you expect?'
My mother: 'You invited him in – what did you expect?'

You were two years gone; I swallowed the hook of his smile
when he coiled a tattooed arm around my waist.
I still feel hands tighten like snares in my sleep.
Damn these numb fists. My gun by the bolted door.

In Amber

They've been coupled fifty million years:
the pair of midges trapped in Baltic amber.
Antennae of the male like thistledown fronds,
the female's gauze wings, her body umber.
She sipped the blood of mousebirds and dawn horses,
he flew to her wingbeats' call. Landing on timber,
they mated – facing opposite ways, yet tender –
now trapped in the pine-tree's tears, liquid embers.

Voyeur with a lens, I spy on what's left of their lust.
Caught in resin, three globes of fossil air:
if I broke them, I could breathe the past.
So why did you give me their long-spent affair
in this gem last May, but leave in December?
I dig out your number – almost type, '*Do you remember?*'

Cairning

A bedstone for each Shetland your grandfather broke
for the pit. One for each injured nag

whose broken-winded throat he sliced.
A rag-rock for each numbered ewe

your father drove to the slaughterman's truck
for cold-shouldering her lambs.

A flagstone for the house overlooking the fold
that I'll never build with you.

A pinning-pebble for the roosting tawny
that won't swivel its head and rivet me with a stare,

a hearting-space for the small hand that won't pull mine
to the nest in the hawthorns to look, look.

A keystone for your name: a shred of blood-striped plaid
reiving over the Tweed to this frosty edge of England.

A capstone for the drovers' path that hugs the border
then jumps the fence for Scotland, to summit Windy Gyle.

I've piled them high, keyed in by their roughness,
their weight. The mound grows, a chip off

those memorials raised by gallowglasses
north of the battlefield, as they limped the long road home.

Of the Flesh

> *I still wanted to free that cry when I painted the beef carcass.*
> *I have not yet succeeded.* – Chaïm Soutine.

The kick of your father's gun –
the shot
sent a buck-rabbit
thrashing in convulsions –
its cry entered me.

You twisted the neck. It lay
abruptly silent. Still,
after three years, I hear the cry.

But I, too, have stripped
the skin like a robe
and slid a hand between the strakes
of ribs, to feel
the still-warm heart.

I have returned
the blank gaze of a peeled head.

But when I saw the creature's arms
thrown wide, baring the emptied chest,
its voice of wire
filled my ears.

That night, an air rifle cracked through sleep
by the sett in the woods
and the cry seized my throat –

broke off, severed
as your fingers stroked my nape in the dark.

Of Desire

My voice must be a chantry, my skin an unstained alb:
this was the creed of my fathers.

The priest sent us to kneel for a man who gripped his crozier.
He stroked our cheeks and offered us wine that bled.

Like as the hart desireth the water-brooks, we sang.
At Passiontide, the padre thundered that women were rib-bones:

The lust of the flesh and the lust of the eyes is not of the Father.
He preached of the Jealous God, Ancient of Days.

But the rood-screen was carved with figs and rose hips,
while the Book told me: *Thy breasts are like two young roes.*

My lover and I walked to a chapel where faces peered from stone leaves.
The priest asked me: *Who is this, that cometh up from the wilderness?*

I answered: *As the apple tree among the wood, so is my beloved
among the sons. His desire is toward me.* We took the path

that winds from the lychgate, to the orchard's chancel.
I told my love: *Let's go early to the vineyards – let's see if the vine has budded.*

Light, Sweet Crude

1

At dawn, my father left to work the seafloor fields.
Between fjords and the Firth, the rig hummed
from its crown-block to the pit of its possum belly.
He grafted with roughnecks and a crude-talking toolpusher:
their toil stoked fuel-lines, fired flarestacks, drove motors.
Farther north, the trickle and tick of ice floes.

That year's gales uprooted dunes, hurled gulls
along Union Street; the derrick strained at its anchors,
weathering the storm-surge.
                                His chair sat empty.
The desk paperweight: a drop of Brent crude
globed in glass, the tarry slick levelled as I tilted it.
I tried to pray for breezes to ferry him home,
but all I could invoke were fields of North Sea oil:
Magnus, Beatrice, Forties, Glenlyon, Loyal.

2

When I was nine, my father made me leave –
he drilled an emirate with straight-ruled borders.
The heat on the runway like the breath of a foundry.
My Narnia books arrived after their voyage
along the Suez Canal, in the sea-freight.
Wearing shorts was forbidden – even for men.

Mirage city, under the warp-shimmer of fifty degrees.
Sun-beaten metal. Light-struck glass,
the bombed-out bridge to Bubiyan Island.
At the sandstone ridge on the edge of Iraq,
they turned camels loose to trigger landmines.

We learnt at school that oil was fossil light:
one barrelful did twelve years' human work.
My father's friends talked Bonny Light, Brent Blend,
Sour Heavy Crude. They measured wealth in barrels.
Oil was refined, but its temper had a flash-point –

3

I'd listen from the landing:

"They kicked down the door
of the neighbours' shop,
then bullets started shattering the windows.
Khalid and I ran.
We saw tanks rolling down Gulf Street.

They stole everything – air conditioners, cigarettes –
then torched the ground floor.
My cousin shot at the police station they'd seized.
They tore out his eyes."

"The burning pipeline howled –
Sara said like a jet engine.
Fire-trenches and oil-lakes under a sky dark at midday.
Six million barrels of light, sweet crude ..."

"I watched birds wading in the slick-ponds.
There was a hoopoe drinking petroleum,
an oiled eagle panting for water."

"Airstrike on the Basra road:
the man clawed at the windscreen,
trying to smash free before the petrol tank blew.
An American camera blinked at his burnt-out sockets."

4

From Anchorage, Calgary, Houston or Galveston,
my father returned, jet-lagged and running fumes,
to plant English lavender on Texan time.
His shirts would smell of earth and gasoline.
I'd see him at the sink, scrubbing his hands:
"I've fixed the engine!" He'd show his palms,
lines stained with viscid oil, the cuticles blackened.
I watched him scouring skin that wouldn't come clean.

A two-stroke heart has steely valves and chambers
but frail fuel-lines. He said he'd hike the path
above the falls, but dusk failed to bring him home –
The spring after we burned him, I piled his books
in a rusty petrol-drum, and struck the match. A pyre
for *Fire in the Night, Offshore, World Oil, Pioneer.*

Muirburn

My father weighed a little less than at birth.
I carried him in both hands to the pines
as October brought the burning season.
When I unscrewed the urn, bone-chaff and grit
streamed out, with their gunpowder smell.
       I remembered the sulphur hiss of the match –
how he taught me to breathe on the steeple of logs
until the kindling caught and flames quickened.

That night, in sleep, I saw the forest clearing
by the moor's edge, and the ring of his ashes.
       A skirl of smoke began to rise –
bracken curling, a fume of blaeberry leaves.
Ants broke their ranks to scatter and flee,
and a moth spun ahead of the fire-wind.
I took the path over the heath at a run.

A voice at my shoulder said, "You'll inherit fire."
And through the smoke I glimpsed a line of figures
on the hillside, beating and beating the heather
as the fire-front roared towards them.
A volley of shouts: "Keep the wind at your back!"
       My grandmother threshing with a fire-broom,
Dad hacking a firebreak. My stillborn brother, now grown,
sprinting for the hollow where the spring once flowed,
the whole hill flaring in the updraft.

And there: a girl, running for the riverside –
she wore my face, the shade of ash.

Things My Father Told Me

The Latin for 'Do your own homework, you bastard'.
That like a bee, a line from Virgil has six feet.

The German for 'Are those sultanas, or do you keep rabbits under the counter?'
King's College pinkos would sell me to the Russians.

Engineers make useful husbands. The way to check tyre pressure.
How to prune vines, willows and cypresses.

A method for telling if Gorms are living in your cairns.
Naismith's rule for pace and gradient.

That in his day, you hiked two hundred and sixty-seven miles
on beer and Kendal mint cake, and were grateful.

Munro charted the Highlands by night, with a darkened lantern.
Wainwright loved his dogs more than his wives.

That he'd staggered down from the summit of Cairngorm,
laden with mountain quartz for my mother.

The Oak Husband

He'll wed me with five hundred years of rings,
my love in lichen and ivy, and give me
his heartwood older than England.
I'll pledge him my budding years,
the slow twining that grows with age.

He'll give me his branches that hold up the sky,
an acorn crown. I ache for stolid earth,
his hushing voice of rain. In my gown
of lilies, I'll rush to the chapel of trees.
The whole village will throng to see us:
the bride and the pride of the forest. I'll live
light as a leaf in the clasp of his limbs –
at the end, they will bury me under his root.

The Lady and the Unicorn

The smell of iron and rawhide whips –
I'd hide in a thicket as the hunt rode by,
a beast unknown to men.

But she stalked the clearings with naked feet.
I'd watch her stroll by the spring each dawn
and feel her gaze tingle along my flanks.

She held an apple: my withers shook,
but my mouth watered for the smell of it.
I took a step, and then a step.

Untamed, new-touched, I shied
at her hand on my forehead,
but bit the fruit: its stinging sweetness.

One morning, she showed me my image
in a glass. White as an icicle, slot-hooved,
the brittle weapon of my horn.

 "You're rare as ivory," she said. "My Will
is a horseman. How he'd love to mount
an unbroken creature like you!

But you'll stay wild, *mon seul désir*."
She wove our portraits in a tapestry
of silver thread, and hung it from a holly.

That June, I sheltered in the shade
of her pavilion with her hound and spaniel.
Her serving-girl offered us berries,

I laid my head in my lady's lap.
From the forest's edge, a lingering breath
on a horn sounded the mort.

Tamer and Gyrfalcon

The wood is fenced. Those fields are walled.
Your horses kick against their stalls.

You show me lures and hoods and gloves,
and say you'll tame me with your love.

I gralloch fawns. I eat raw fox.
I won't stay caged within this box.

You clamp a ring to my scaly thigh
and bind my ankles. *Go on, fly!*

My feet are scythes. My face an axe.
Pray that when you call, I don't come back.

Peregrines

Peregrine (adjective) – coming from another country.

We thought it was the catch of breath that forecasts heavy weather:
something restive in the leaves, the weathercocks in a spin.

When nightingales called *cheer-up, jug-jug*, the grouse cried out *go-back*;
the hedgerows emptied quickly, in a gale of fleeing wings.

In the spring, a leaflet fluttered through each letterbox:
Even the blackbirds in your garden came from Eastern Europe.

Lairds ordered the gamekeepers to spare goshawks and harriers,
and fix their crosshairs on migrant snowy owls.

Brent geese wheeled north, oaring the air for Svalbard;
fieldfares left their seafaring, turned tail for the fjords.

A mob in Oxford doused the swallows' nests with DDT –
poachers of French partridges escaped, never prosecuted.

The whole sky dark with them – a rain of down and droppings.
A year with a silent summer, and our islands cast adrift.

My grandmother's ashes stirred beneath a Sussex apple tree,
restless for the crossing home to Chemin des Fauconniers.

I could only name my estrangement in words with distant origins –
all that was peregrine in me quivered to take flight.

La Pive

I've often transplanted it
from Valais woods to foreign forests:
my grandmother's word for a fir cone.

The Académie française would scowl
at this word used by Swiss *paysans*.
Even the dictionary shows me its *correcteur*

then tells me that in France, *le pive*
is a bullfinch, or slang for house red.
La pive – the feminine – a dunce.

A peasants' word? Pine is *sapin*
in the most cultured French.
Sappos in earthy Gaulish, crossed with

pinus: the imperious Latin stem.
I cultivate these branches
and plantings of the tongue:

can trace *pive* back to Sanskrit,
the scripture of the Vedas –
its taproot: *pit*, meaning resin.

My grandmother showed me how summer
unlocks the bracts of *pives*, loosing a swarm
of pips, each with its single wing.

She'd point to a nurse-log, burdened with seedlings,
or a hacked stump in a grove
caulking its wound, and live at the roots.

Wayfarers
Translation of 'Des passants' by Philippe Jaccottet

We won't meet again on these roads –
won't even see our dead again,
nor their shadows.
                      Their bodies, their shades
and memories are ash. A faceless wind
scatters it; nothing can withstand it.
                 All the same,
we still hear their bird-cries
under clouds, as we trek through the silence
of an empty October noon –
their calls both distant and close.

They're getting rarer, as the cold
rolls in on its raincart like dusk.
They span the sky.
                    I walk beneath them,
and it seems that they've not questioned or called –
but replied, beneath the low October clouds.

Spikenard

I trailed your flint and bayleaf scent to the porch,
but someone else's perfume was mixed with yours –

coiling with jonquils, spikenard, and something musky.
I paused at your alderwood door.

You were wreathed in the cologne I bought you:
Terre. Its heart-chord silex and bitter orange,

the base-note (which lingers longest) is Atlas cedar.
I remembered how I'd settle my cheek on your chest

to feel the stroke of your heart, until your fragrance
steeped my pores, and I'd breathe you in for weeks.

I pictured her hands at your belt, in that attic room –
my key still sprang the bolt.

Acknowledgements

I would like to thank the Poetry Society for the inaugural Peggy Poole Award, and Deryn Rees-Jones for her brilliant mentoring as part of the award. Before that, the Jerwood/Arvon mentoring scheme and Pascale Petit gave me the courage to explore challenging themes in my poetry.

Special thanks go to Carol Ann Duffy, Gillian Clarke and Ty Newydd, for their transformative Laureates' Masterclass, which helped me to write some of these poems.

Poems have appeared previously in the 2018 National Poetry Competition winners' anthology, *The North*, the *Midnight Listening* Jerwood/Arvon mentees' anthology, and on the Poetry School's website.

'Firesetter' received the top poetry prize at the 2018 Creative Futures Literary Awards and was published in their anthology *Chemistry*.